SPORTS INJURIES:
HOW TO PREVENT, DIAGNOSE, & TREAT

GYMNASTICS

Sports Injuries:
How to Prevent, Diagnose, & Treat

- Baseball
- Basketball
- Cheerleading
- Equestrian
- Extreme Sports
- Field
- Field Hockey
- Football
- Gymnastics
- Hockey
- Ice Skating
- Lacrosse
- Soccer
- Track
- Volleyball
- Weight Training
- Wrestling

SPORTS INJURIES:
HOW TO PREVENT, DIAGNOSE, & TREAT

GYMNASTICS

CHRIS McNAB

MASON CREST PUBLISHERS
www.masoncrest.com

Mason Crest Publishers Inc.
370 Reed Road
Broomall, PA 19008
(866) MCP-BOOK (toll free)
www.masoncrest.com

First printing

1 2 3 4 5 6 7 8 9 10

Library of Congress Cataloging-in-Publication Data on file
at the Library of Congress

ISBN 1-59084-633-8

Series ISBN 1-59084-625-7

Editorial and design by
Amber Books Ltd.
Bradley's Close
74–77 White Lion Street
London N1 9PF
www.amberbooks.co.uk

Project Editor: Michael Spilling
Design: Graham Curd
Picture Research: Natasha Jones

Printed and bound in the Hashemite Kingdom of Jordan

PICTURE CREDITS
Corbis: 6, 8, 10, 11, 13, 14, 15, 16, 18, 21, 22, 24, 26, 28, 32, 34, 36, 37, 39, 52, 55, 59; ©**EMPICS**: 40, 43, 44; **PA Photos**: 56.

FRONT COVER: All ©EMPICS, except Corbis (bl).

ILLUSTRATIONS: Courtesy of Amber Books except:
Bright Star Publishing plc: 49, 51.

CONTENTS

Foreword

Sports Injuries: How to Prevent, Diagnose, and Treat is a seventeen-volume series written for young people who are interested in learning about various sports and how to participate in them safely. Each volume examines the history of the sport and the rules of play; it also acts as a guide for prevention and treatment of injuries, and includes instruction on stretching, warming up, and strength training, all of which can help players avoid the most common musculoskeletal injuries. *Sports Injuries* offers ways for readers to improve their performance and gain more enjoyment from playing sports, and young athletes will find these volumes informative and helpful in their pursuit of excellence.

Sports medicine professionals assigned to a sport that they are not familiar with can also benefit from this series. For example, a football athletic trainer may need to provide medical care for a local gymnastics meet. Although the emergency medical principles and action plan would remain the same, the athletic trainer could provide better care for the gymnasts after reading a simple overview of the principles of gymnastics in *Sports Injuries*.

Although these books offer an overview, they are not intended to be comprehensive in the recognition and management of sports injuries. The text helps the reader appreciate and gain awareness of the common injuries possible during participation in sports. Reference material and directed readings are provided for those who want to delve further into the subject.

Written in a direct and easily accessible style, *Sports Injuries* is an enjoyable series that will help young people learn about sports and sports medicine.

Susan Saliba, Ph.D., National Athletic Trainers' Association Education Council

A gymnast, wearing wrist supports to protect his wrists from injury, performs a technique on the pommel horse.

History

To find the origins of gymnastics, we must go back 2,000 years to the world of ancient Greece. Its philosophers, including Plato and Aristotle, promoted the idea that a strong, supple body helped develop a clear and powerful mind.

Greek intellectuals used to gather in a gymnasium for debating and philosophizing, as well as physical exercise. Gymnastics—those exercises that were performed in a gymnasium—initially meant any technique of body conditioning, including wrestling, running, and even boxing. All athletes exercised naked, and from this comes the word "gymnastics," which derives from the Greek word *gymnos,* meaning naked.

The world's first Olympic games, held in 776 B.C.E. in Olympia, Greece, featured only one sport, running. Subsequent Olympics introduced other gymnastic events, but did not contain gymnastics in the form we know today. In the second century B.C.E., Greece was swallowed by the mighty Roman Empire, and the Olympics degenerated, becoming little more than violent entertainment: the most popular spectacles were the bloody gladiatorial fights. Finally, in 393 C.E., two factors combined to bring the Olympics to an end: a series of financial scandals within the games and the rise of Christianity, a religion that did not promote worship of the human form. Competitive gymnastics seemed destined to disappear altogether.

Nadia Comaneci delivers a gold-medal winning performance on the beam. Comaneci became perhaps the most famous gymnast in history during the 1970s and was a household name.

THE REVIVAL

They would have disappeared, were it not for two men in the nineteenth century, the German, Friedrich Ludwig Jahn (1778–1839) and the Swede, Per Henrik Ling (1776–1839). Jahn's contribution was perhaps the most important.

During the early part of the nineteenth century, physical competition became fashionable in Europe once again, particularly among military forces. In this climate, Jahn—a schoolmaster by profession—invented the exercises and also the exercise apparatus that would become central to modern gymnastics. This equipment included the **parallel bars**, the **vaulting horse**, the **rings**, and the **horizontal bar**.

An ancient European mosaic shows a gymnast in training. Gymnastics in classical Greece and Rome were as much about developing the mind as the body.

Jahn also organized gymnasts into *turneveins,* associations for the practice of gymnastics. These were exported to the United States by German emigrants in the nineteenth and twentieth centuries and became the foundations of modern gymnastic associations.

While Jahn developed equipment-based gymnastics, Ling developed routines based on fluid and expressive body movements alone, and these techniques would lead to the phenomenon of **rhythmic gymnastics**.

Gymnastics flourished in schools, sports clubs, and various other institutions across Europe during the

A picture of gymnasts from Czechoslovakia in Eastern Europe exercising on the rings in the early twentieth century. An army officer looks on—many athletes were serving as soldiers at this time.

1800s, and from the 1830s in the United States (where the first official gymnastic club was established in 1850). The sport was also organized into official controlling bodies. The *Fédération Internationale Gymnastique* (**FIG**) became the chief European body in 1881. In the United Kingdom, the British Amateur Gymnastics Association (AGA) was formed in 1888, while in the United States, the Amateur Athletic Union (AAU) oversaw gymnastics from 1883.

In 1896, gymnastics made a triumphant return to the world stage, forming an integral part of the reborn Olympic Games. Appropriately, these were held in

Athens, where gymnastics was born. Events included vaulting, **pommel horse**, rings, parallel bars, and horizontal bar, and by 1924 athletes were competing for individual titles on each piece of apparatus, as well as for overall medals for a team's combined exercises. From 1928, women gymnasts were able to compete in the Olympics, but only for team titles in the disciplines of vault, **beam, asymmetric bars**, and **floor exercise**. Women were not allowed to compete for individual titles across the full range of events in the same way as men until 1952.

MODERN GYMNASTICS

Modern gymnastics has settled into two main categories: classic gymnastics and rhythmic sportive gymnastics. Classic gymnastics involves traditional equipment-based routines. For men, this means parallel bars, **high bar**, rings, pommel horse, and vault (with the vaulting horse arranged lengthwise), as well as floor exercise. For women, the events are floor exercise, asymmetric bars, beam, and vault (with the box arranged across the path of approach).

Rhythmic gymnastics involves dancelike athletic routines on a mat, using hand-held equipment such as ribbons, balls, and hoops. The equipment is controlled to illustrate the fluidity and grace of the gymnast's body movements. Rhythmic gymnastics can be performed by individuals or by teams demonstrating synchronized patterns. It originated in the 1930s, but was not accepted by the FIG until 1962. In 1964, rhythmic gymnastics was featured in the World Gymnastic Championships and was accepted as an individual event in the Olympic Games in 1984.

FAMOUS GYMNASTS

During the early days of gymnastics in the late eighteenth and early nineteenth centuries, Western European gymnasts were the most successful. Germany,

France, Switzerland, Italy, and Sweden produced the world leaders in the sport. The United States did step onto the medals podium when Anton Heist won five gold medals and a silver at the 1904 Olympics in St. Louis, and the remarkable George Eyser, who had a wooden leg, won the parallel bars event during the same games. It should be noted, however, that the United States was the only country to compete in the gymnastics section of the 1904 Olympics.

Although some gymnasts achieved local fame, it was not until sporting events began to be televised in the 1960s and 1970s that certain gymnasts became household names, particularly those originating from Communist Europe, the United States, and Japan.

A female gymnast from Denmark, Europe, competes in London on the beam during the 1920s/1930s. Women were not able to enter Olympic gymnastics until 1928.

In 1972, the Soviet gymnast Olga Korbut astonished the world by winning three gold medals and a silver medal at the 1972 Olympics in Munich, Germany. Even Korbut, however, was overshadowed by possibly the most famous gymnast of all time, Nadia Comaneci of Romania. Born in 1961, Comaneci began training in gymnastics at the age of six, winning her first junior championship when she was only nine. Her crowning moment came at the 1976 Olympics, when she took gold in the asymmetric bars with a perfect score of 10.00, a score then unheard of in gymnastics. She went on to win many more medals.

From the 1980s on, the United States became more of a force in gymnastics. Mary Lou Retton won five gold medals at the 1984 Olympics in Los Angeles and was entered into the U.S. Olympic Hall of Fame a year later. At the same Olympics, Bart Connor won two gold medals (team event and parallel bars), despite having a torn biceps. In the 1990s, Shannon Miller won three gold medals at the 1993 World Championships in Birmingham, England, and two gold medals at the World Championships in Australia the next year. More recently, U.S. National Champion Sean Townsend won a gold medal in the parallel bars at the 2001 World Championships, becoming the first U.S. athlete to win a gold medal in the World Championships since 1979.

Nadia Comaneci celebrates after being awarded a perfect 10.00—a score never before seen in gymnastics—during the 1976 summer Olympics held in Montreal, Canada.

PARALLEL BARS AND ASYMMETRIC BARS

The parallel bars and asymmetric bars are two of the oldest pieces of apparatus used in modern gymnastics. Parallel bars were invented by Friedrich Jahn and have been part of the Olympic program since 1896. They are used to demonstrate swinging, vaulting, and balancing movements, which require immense upper-body strength. The asymmetric bars were first introduced into gymnastic programs in 1936 and are exclusive to women's competition. A gymnast using the asymmetric bars will perform routines involving complex swinging and hanging motions, often bending her body around the lower bar at high speeds.

A Soviet gymnast receives instruction in the parallel bars from his coach at a training center in Moscow. Both parallel and asymmetric bars require enormous development of the shoulder and arm muscles.

Mental Preparation to Avoid Injury

Gymnastics requires an amazing control over the human physique. Yet to help avoid the injuries that plague many athletes, the mind must be prepared as well as the body.

The connection between physical safety and mental training might not seem obvious, but it is vital. Any athlete who is mentally tired, self-conscious, afraid, or embarrassed will be distracted and lacking in confidence when performing a technique. If the technique happens to be, for example, a complex vault, any lapse in concentration may be disastrous, resulting in serious injury. Consequently, most reputable coaches and gyms will emphasize mental training as part of their safety program.

POSITIVE FEEDBACK

The first, and possibly most important, step in mental training is to find the right coach. Visit a gym before you actually join, and check for the following signs:

- A friendly but professional atmosphere among the staff and pupils;
- A high standard of equipment, all in good working order;
- Trainers with a safety certification from U.S.A. Gymnastics;

Beam exercises require exceptional concentration from the gymnast. She must never lose a sense of where the beam is, as a mistake of only a few inches can result in severe injury.

A good coach is important for your self-esteem as well as your training. He or she should give you positive feedback on your performance and help you to bounce back after mistakes.

- A busy program of events, competitions, and social activities. The more activities there are, the more likely it is that the staff are dedicated to excellence.

Signs such as these indicate a reputable club, where you can be confident of good teaching. Make sure that you and your parents do as much checking as possible into the background of the club and its staff before you begin training.

Your coach is central to your mental confidence. A good coach will give you frequent positive feedback about what you are doing; will never embarrass you or make you feel inferior; and, most importantly, will provide clear and understandable training, taking you forward in steady and manageable steps. Even if you are a naturally talented gymnast, do not try to push yourself ahead of your coach's teaching. Safe gymnastics requires a good grasp of all the basic techniques. Trying advanced techniques before you are truly ready puts you in serious danger of injury.

Remember to help your coach to help you. Ask about anything that you do not understand, and do not attempt any exercise or technique without knowing exactly what you are doing. Above all, never go into a technique feeling afraid of hurting yourself. Gymnastics should be performed with total confidence. Anything less and you are at risk of having an accident because fear will make your body movements weak and uncertain. Your coach will go a long way to helping you find this confidence, but what can you do for yourself?

MENTAL TRAINING

The first stage in mental training is to take charge of your inner voice. Instead of thinking thoughts that criticize your performance—such as "I'll never be good enough" or "This is too difficult"—think positive thoughts. For example, when performing a difficult **salto** technique, try saying to yourself, "I'm getting better every time I practice this" or "Nothing will stop me from mastering this technique." Even if you do not quite believe what you are saying, keep at it. You will soon find that positive thinking becomes a habit that breeds the confidence needed to perform good gymnastic techniques. If you do find yourself thinking a negative thought, immediately counteract it with a positive one. Keep doing this until positive thinking becomes a habit.

If there are areas in your life outside the gym which are troubling or depressing you, try to deal with these first. Otherwise, such problems will still be on your mind when training and may lead to lapses in concentration and accidents. Talk to your parents and coach about these problems, and tackle them with the same commitment and positive focus you bring to your sport.

When it comes to improving your technique, there should be several elements to your mental training. Gymnastics requires a high level of concentration, so much of your mental training should aim at developing 100 percent focus. Practice the following concentration exercises, both recommended by senior gymnastics instructors:

1. Memorizing cards

The use of memorizing cards is a classic mental training activity. Lay five playing cards down in front of you, face up. Memorize the cards one at a time, turning each face down as you work along the line of cards. When all are face down, wait five minutes, and then try to remember the cards in sequence, stating what you think each card is before turning it over to see if you are right. Repeat this challenge with an increasing number of cards, thus stretching your power to concentrate and focus.

Establish a fixed warm-up routine for use at every competition. It will not only prepare your body, but also focus your mind on what lies ahead of you and help to control nervousness.

2. Focus on breathing

Sit in a quiet place and close your eyes, then focus all your attention on the sound and feel of your breathing. Breathe slowly and deliberately, pulling air in through your nose until the lungs are full, then expelling it slowly through the mouth. When you first practice this, you will find that your concentration will start to drift after only a few seconds. Do not berate yourself for this; simply bring your attention back to your breathing. With practice, you will be able to maintain the concentration for many minutes, even hours, and your concentration will be much strengthened.

MENTAL FOCUS IN COMPETITIONS

More serious injuries occur during competitions than in training. The following are tips to help you control nerves during competition:

- Make sure that you pack every item of equipment you need before you set off for the competition. Forgetting something will increase anxiety and lower confidence. Also, arrive at the place of the competition in plenty of time.

- If possible, warm up gently in the competition hall itself. Get used to the noise of the crowd, the lighting, and general environment.

- Visualize yourself performing the routine in the competition hall. See yourself moving with confidence and strength.

- If you are at the competition all day, eat a small, light lunch, such as a pasta or rice dish accompanied by fruit. Avoid large and meaty meals, which will make you feel sluggish.

- Try to enjoy yourself, and show the judges what you can do.

Pasta is an excellent energy food. Unlike sugary snacks, which give only a quick burst of energy, it will release its energy over a long period of time.

Professional athletes in many sports now use a technique called visualization to improve their physical performance. Here's how it works. Say you are learning a difficult handspring vault. Sitting quietly, close your eyes, then picture yourself doing the vault perfectly. Open the power of your imagination: imagine the sights and sounds of the gym as vividly as possible, and try to feel the movement of your muscles as you whip through the air during the handspring. See the smooth lines of flight your body takes, and feel a sense of balance as you land.

Scientific research has shown that when the brain imagines performing an action in detail, the body learns that action as if it were actually training physically. Visualization cannot replace physical training, but it can help your body to learn the techniques more quickly and also improve your gymnastic confidence. Practice it regularly, at least once a week, and concentrate on visualizing the techniques which make you the most nervous.

HIT THE BOOKS

One final way of preparing your mind for gymnastics is by reading about it. Read as much about gymnastics as you can, everything from biographies of its legendary sportsmen and women to books helping you to master techniques. Reading about the sport will help you to find more enthusiasm to practice hard and may also warn you of dangers in your technique. One caution—if an instructional book teaches you very different methods from your coach, stick with the coach's methods. Your coach is on hand to ensure your safety during training, whereas an author is not.

By treating gymnastics as both a mental and physical challenge, you can experience the strength and success that come from a disciplined, focused mind. Such a mind will stand you in good stead for life, both inside and outside the gymnasium.

Warming Up

Any gymnast about to exercise must warm up first. Raising muscle temperature and flexibility through light exercise and stretching helps to prevent injury and gives the body a greater range of movement.

A thorough warm-up before exercise is important, because cold muscles are more susceptible to injury than warm ones. A cold muscle is stiffer and has a shorter range of movement. It also has a greater risk of tearing or straining when put under sudden and strenuous movement. A proper warm-up consists of two elements: light exercise to raise the body temperature, followed by stretching.

LIGHT EXERCISE

The exercise period of a warm-up is aimed at raising body temperature and loosening up muscles. It should not be too vigorous—just a series of light, gentle exercises to raise the heart rate and breathing rate slightly and prepare muscles for harder exercise. As a gymnast, however, you need to do some warm-ups specific to your sport to help prevent common gymnastic injuries. The ankles and wrists are the most commonly injured parts of a gymnast's body, suffering mainly from acute sprains during falls or impacts with equipment.

To warm up the wrists, first shake them lightly and then circle the hands while keeping the forearms still. Circle in one direction for about twenty seconds, then

A young gymnast makes a static position on the rings. Without a full warm-up, this athlete would be at risk of sprains and strains in the shoulders and arms, and injuries to lower limbs after dismounting.

A young gymnast works on her back flexibility. Outside of the gymnasium, it is vital that the gymnast has good posture when sitting, standing, and lifting in order to avoid back injuries.

the reverse. Next, bend the hands backward and forward to their fullest extent, switching directions about once every second for about twenty seconds.

Now focus on the ankles. Put one hand against a wall for balance, then lift one leg from the floor and circle the foot around, warming up the ankle joint. Reverse the direction of the circles, then repeat the exercise using the other foot. Finally, push and pull each ankle backward and forward, repeating the two movements about ten times.

Following this sequence of exercises, your muscles should be warmed up and less at risk of injury. Now you should begin to stretch.

STRETCHING

Why is stretching important to prevent injury? Stretching maximizes the body's range of movement by progressively lengthening the muscles. When a gymnast

WARM-UP

Warm-up exercise routines vary from sport to sport and from coach to coach. The following is an example only:

1. Walk quickly around the gym or jog very lightly on the spot. Do this for a few minutes until you begin to feel warmer.

2. Spend a few minutes doing a moderately strenuous exercise such as star jumps or lunges. Do not, however, push yourself too hard, as your muscles still have a lot of warming up to do.

3. Stand still with your legs shoulder-width apart, feet facing forward. Swing your arms gently in wide circles, first forward for about twenty seconds, then backward for another twenty seconds.

4. In the same position, put your hands on your hips and rotate the hips in large circles. After about twenty seconds, reverse the direction of the circles.

5. Stand up straight with your arms held out loosely in front of you. Twist your upper body gently around to your left as far as you can comfortably go, and hold it in this position for about ten seconds. Then repeat the exercise for the opposite side. Do a complete set of movements three times.

After these exercises, you should be feeling warmer and looser.

performs a jumping split, for example, all the muscle groups and **ligaments** of the legs and hips are stretched to their fullest extent. If the gymnast is not flexible, the sudden strain will take the muscle fibers beyond their capability and probably result in torn muscles or other tissues. Stretching is designed to lengthen the muscles and so enable such movements. It also benefits the gymnast by reducing the possibilities of sprains and helping sore and stiff muscles recover from heavy workouts.

This stretch improves the flexibility of the calf muscles and hamstrings. The torso must be kept facing forward throughout the stretch.

There are literally hundreds of stretches available to help the gymnast achieve maximum flexibility. Your coach should be able to teach you specific techniques appropriate to your chosen gymnastic specialty. Here we will look at the general principles of stretching and how to make sure that stretching itself does not result in injury.

All stretching works by elongating muscles and ligaments and also by reducing the muscles' tendency to tighten and contract when stretched.

BALLISTIC STRETCHING

Ballistic stretching is performed with vigorous bouncing or jerking movements. It is a technique that is now discouraged by most trainers. The jerking movements involved in ballistic stretching can easily result in damaged muscles or ligaments because these stretches do not build up flexibility gradually and safely.

RESISTANCE STRETCHING

Resistance stretching is often performed with a partner. It generally uses what is known as the "Contract–Relax" (CR) technique. For example, to stretch the **hamstrings**, a gymnast lies down on her back and places one leg on the shoulder of a partner, who is kneeling in a supporting position. She then contracts her hamstring muscles tightly, and pushes against his shoulder, holding this tension for up to fifteen seconds. Then she relaxes and, at the same time, her partner gently pushes her leg up toward her face. This process is then repeated several times, each time advancing the leg further into the stretch.

Resistance stretching works on the principle that a relaxed muscle stretches better than a tense muscle. The sudden relaxation of the tense muscle provides the ideal moment for an efficient stretch. Resistance stretching is certainly a very effective technique. The only problem can be that you might stretch further than you should and subsequently pull or tear the muscle.

Warm up the shoulders by rotating the arms around in large circles, reversing the direction after about ten full swings.

29

WHEN NOT TO STRETCH

Do not perform stretching exercises if:

- **You are suffering from a muscle injury in the area you want to stretch;**
- **You are recovering from a bone fracture, unless stretching is part of a program of physical therapy;**
- **You find you are becoming less rather than more flexible, which could indicate an illness or disease;**
- **You have an inflamed joint, or the joint is unstable from an injury;**
- **You experience sudden intense pain when attempting to stretch.**

STATIONARY STRETCHING

This is the most common type of flexibility training. It involves stretching to the point at which tension is felt, then holding the position for up to ten seconds to enable the muscles to relax into the stretch and lengthen. The side split is a typical example of a stationary stretch. The athlete lowers his torso toward the ground, supporting much of his body weight on his hands, while opening his legs out in a wide "A" shape. When he senses he has reached the limit of his stretching capability, he stops and tries to relax the leg muscles for about ten seconds. After this, he may find that he can stretch even further and is able to repeat the push, hold, relax sequence. Once the stretch is completed, the athlete then gently pulls himself out of it.

Regardless of the type of stretching or warm-up routine, obey these general rules:

- Always stop immediately if you feel any sudden pain or burning sensations.
- Stop if you feel nauseous, faint, or ill in any way.

Holding this position for about three seconds stretches the hamstrings of the extended leg. Slide into the position slowly, and release gently. Repeat three times on each leg.

• Keep breathing deeply throughout any stretch—your muscles need good supplies of oxygen to cope with the effort.

• Make sure that you stretch after you have completed your day's exercise. The muscles, which will be tired and sore from overwork, recover more quickly if they are stretched as the body is cooling down.

Stretching prevents the muscles from tightening up and becoming stiff.

One final point about your preparation for gymnastics is that flexible muscles also need to be strong muscles. A sensible weight-training regime should be as much a part of your routine as flexibility exercises. Weight training needs special supervision for people under the age of eighteen. Your coach should be able to give you all the information you need.

Tricep dips are excellent for improving the strength of the upper arms and shoulders. Bend until the upper arm is parallel to the ground.

Equipment and Training

The type of equipment available, and how you use it, has an important impact on your likelihood of being injured during training. Some simple precautions and checks can reduce the risk.

Modern equipment has made the sport of gymnastics much safer than it used to be. Until the mid-1960s, for example, gymnastic floor mats were made of a combination of horsehair and straw. During heavy landings, such mats provided minimal cushioning, and serious ankle, knee, and back injuries were commonplace. As for other equipment, balance beams were constructed of hard, slippery wood. Asymmetric bars were also wooden and could shatter if grabbed while they were vibrating.

Today, all this has changed. Floor mats are now made of thick urethane covered with polyethylene or vinyl, and they provide substantial support during landings. Balance beams are constructed from modern slip-resistant plastics, and they also feature foam padding to lessen impact injuries. Asymmetric bars are made of fiberglass, which is an immensely strong material and less rigid than wood. Such technological advances have improved the safety of almost all modern gyms and reduced equipment-related injuries.

An amazing display of talent on the pommel horse. The outer surface of the pommel horse must be kept free of cracked or split fabric, which could cause a fall during a routine such as this.

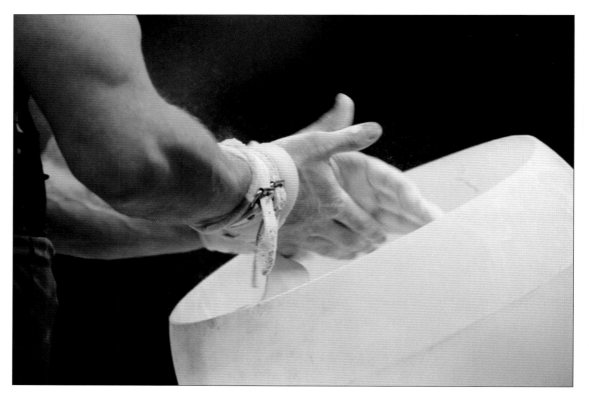

Gymnast's chalk absorbs sweat from the hands and gives the athlete a better grip on equipment such as the pommel horse and rings. Apply the chalk immediately before using the equipment.

EQUIPMENT CHECK

Unless you have gym facilities at home, making sure that gym equipment is well maintained is usually not your responsibility. Your coach should ensure that all facilities are kept in good repair and are set up properly. However, it is wise to be aware of a few points of equipment safety:

• Check that floor mats are securely fastened down and do not slip or shift as they are used. If a large area is covered with mats for floor exercises, make sure that there are no gaps between mats—these can easily produce a sprained ankle if they catch a gymnast's foot during a routine.

- Check that the pieces of equipment are set well apart so that there is no danger of collision with other athletes.
- Worn or damaged equipment should always be replaced or mended. Report any loose nuts, bolts, or other fastenings immediately to your coach, and do not use the equipment until everything is secure. The same applies to any cables or ropes showing signs of fraying, stretching, or cuts.
- Where Velcro is used to secure any equipment, it should be clean of lint to make sure that it grips strongly. Remove lint by cleaning with a stiff brush.

PERSONAL GYM EQUIPMENT

Personal gym equipment is your responsibility, and it is up to you to ensure that you use only items that are safe. Gymnastics is a relatively cheap sport in terms of basic equipment and dress. Girls should wear leotards with no feet. If T-shirts and shorts are worn over the leotard during training, be sure that there is no loose or flapping material that could get caught on equipment. Equipment for boys consists of shorts (or sweat pants) and T-shirts or gym vests. All gymnastic clothing must be free of fastenings such as buttons, zippers, studs, and belts, and the tightening cords of shorts should be tucked inside the waistband.

One important thing to remember is your hair. If you have long hair, tie it back with a hair band only—headbands are prone to getting caught on equipment.

The only shoes worn inside the gym are training shoes. Never wear your training shoes outside the gym because you will end up taking grit back into the gym, damaging floor surfaces and equipment. Gymnastic shoes are specially designed to cushion the ankles and feet against the repeated impacts of training. They also have excellent rubber grip features on the soles to prevent slipping during vaulting or floor routines. Be sure the shoes are fitted properly (your gym

A group of young Chinese gymnasts trains in balancing techniques. Always make sure that there are plenty of people assisting you when you try a technique for the first time on unfamiliar equipment.

shoes may be as much as two sizes bigger than your everyday shoes). If ordering the shoes by mail, some suppliers request that you send a tracing of your foot so the correct size can be sent. Gym shoes are relatively inexpensive. Beginner's shoes can be purchased for between twenty and forty dollars.

Finally, your gym bag should contain any safety equipment that you require for training or competitions. Unless it is supplied at the gym, keep your own supply of gymnast's chalk to reduce sweating on the hands and feet, thus improving your grip. If you have weak or injured joints that need protecting, wear approved ankle, knee, elbow, or wrist supports. For training on the rings, parallel bars, or

The frame, cables, connectors, and rings of this piece of equipment have to withstand tons of pressure. The cables must have no frayed strands, and the rings must be free from cracks or dents.

asymmetric bars, wear properly fitted hand grips. Get your coach or a trained gym supplier to measure you so that you get a product suited to your hand length. The grips are measured from the longest finger to the base of the palm.

SAFE TRAINING

All the safety equipment in the world will make no difference if you fail to follow safe training procedures. The first principle above all is that you learn basic skills before progressing to more difficult techniques. Follow your coach's training regime, and do not attempt any techniques unless your coach or another qualified trainer is present. A **spotter** must always be present, to watch and guide you during techniques. Sometimes the spotter will literally help you to execute techniques by physical manipulation, such as guiding you over the vaulting horse. At other times, verbal guidance will be enough.

Use any safety apparatus available while learning potentially dangerous techniques (particularly vaults) or while learning routines on high pieces of equipment or the trampoline. (Remember, trampoline accidents are the leading cause of paralysis in gymnastics.) A professional gym should be equipped with safety harnesses. These strap to the body and prevent you from falling if you make a mistake.

A good gym will also have graded levels of landing area for those learning to vault. When learning techniques from scratch, landings should take place in deep foam pits. As the technique becomes more familiar, the gymnast can progress to thick crash mats and finally to competition-standard landing mats.

Finally, keep competitions in perspective. Try to concentrate more on enjoying your gymnastics than on winning events. The irony is that by doing this, you will relax and probably win more events anyway.

GYMNASTICS INJURY STATISTICS

- More than 86,000 gymnastics-related injuries are treated in U.S. medical centers every year.
- More than 25,000 gymnasts injured each year are under the age of fifteen.
- Fifty-six percent of high-school gymnasts suffer injuries from training.
- Around thirty-three percent of injuries are experienced by athletes who have already injured themselves on a prior occasion.
- Injuries are three times more likely to occur in competitions than they are in practice.

Good coaching is the most vital element in injury prevention in gymnastics.

Common Injuries and their Treatment

Injury is an extremely serious issue in gymnastics. As many as forty percent of dedicated amateur and professional gymnasts will have to give up their sport eventually because of injury.

Even if a gymnast does not have to give up because of injury, recent studies have shown that at least fifty percent of gymnasts have an injury that has never fully recovered and causes them significant pain.

COMMON INJURIES

Gymnastic injuries occur in two ways: as a result of a specific accident, such as spraining an ankle when landing badly during a vault; or as a result of gradual wear and tear—for example, a gymnast training on a pommel horse might suffer painful, stiff, or inflamed wrists after several months of training as his joints slowly fail to cope with the extreme pressures. The two types of injury occur in roughly equal proportions.

In both men and women, the most common injuries are sprains, muscle strains, bruising, and inflammation (the swelling of muscles or joints). The parts of the body most susceptible to these vary between men and women. Female gymnasts

A gymnast nurses an injured wrist. Wrist injuries usually occur during falls from pieces of equipment or excessive twisting motions during routines such as the floor exercise.

suffer primarily from injuries of the feet, ankles, knees, hands, wrists, and elbows. Male gymnasts also suffer from these injuries, but have a higher incidence of back and shoulder injuries. These result from the uniquely male events—the rings, parallel bars, and pommel horse.

SPRAINS

Sprains occur when a joint is twisted with force in an unnatural direction, resulting in painful and swollen ligaments. Some sprains are serious if the ligaments are completely ruptured by the trauma. Even when the injury has healed, the athlete may experience discomfort and pain in the joint for many years to come.

The most common parts of the body to be sprained are the ankles, knees, and wrists. Symptoms for both are basically the same. Following an accident in which the joint is twisted, the joint swells up and becomes extremely painful whenever pressure is put on it. The joint often appears bruised and is very tender to the touch, and limb mobility is dramatically reduced.

On-the-spot treatment for a sprain is as follows:

- Stop using the joint immediately.
- Rest the joint in the most comfortable position, supported on a cushion.
- Wrap the joint in a **cold compress** to further reduce the swelling and pain, then wrap it with soft padding and bandage it firmly in place. Alternatively, use a compression bandage, which grips the injury quite tightly.
- In the case of a severely sprained ankle, the final stage is to raise the leg on a chair or other surface—this reduces the blood flow to the ankle and lessens swelling.

After immediate treatment, the healing process can begin. If the sprain is acute, professional medical treatment may be required, usually leading to **physical therapy** or, in the worst cases, surgery. For common sprains, rest the joint as much as possible, and do not attempt anything strenuous for at least a week. Keep applying cold compresses three or four times a day, but for no more than twenty minutes at a time because of the danger of localized frostbite.

After about a week, gradually start to move the joint around as it heals, exploring the joint's full range of movement (**R.O.M.**). For example, circle a sprained ankle gently, reversing the direction after every few turns. Draw the ankle backward and forward to free up its vertical movement. The aim is to reintroduce flexibility into the joint. Once you have the full R.O.M. in an injured joint, reintroduce light weight exercises to strengthen it. Do undemanding walks to restore a sprained ankle. Try some light weight training with small dumbbells to work a sprained elbow. If your activities cause you severe pain, however, stop and consult your doctor, physical therapist, or coach.

A slight sprain will usually take around one week to heal, and serious sprains up to two months. Return to training gradually. For the first few

Repeating movements such as these time and time again can result in gradual injuries to the wrists, elbows, and shoulders.

Ankles are commonly injured from falls or awkward landings after dismounts. A severe ankle strain can prevent training for up to three months.

sessions, avoid exercises that are hard on the injured joint. Wear an elasticized joint support to provide extra protection. Once the joint is fully recovered, ask your doctor or coach about exercises to strengthen the ankles or wrists to help prevent further injuries. If, however, the sprain is still problematic after six months, return to your doctor.

The immediate treatment for sprains can be used on many other "soft tissue" injuries, such as pulled muscles, ligaments, and bruising. For muscle strains—a very common injury for gymnasts—rest and apply ice to the injury for the first couple of days. After this, use some of the heat ointments that are available and do some light stretching exercises to restore circulation to the injured muscle. However, if you are in an unusual degree of pain when you injure yourself, you should always consult a doctor or even call the paramedics. This is certainly the case if you suspect broken or dislocated bones.

FRACTURES AND DISLOCATIONS

Fractures occur when the force of impact on a bone is too much for the bone to withstand, and it breaks. **Dislocations** occur when a joint such as a knee or shoulder is pushed out of its normal position. They usually happen when a limb is suddenly wrenched or if the muscles make a very violent contraction, such as when we grasp for something when falling.

Fractures and dislocations among gymnasts are relatively rare, but they do happen because of the physiological stress of the sport. For example, the landing force of a gymnast dismounting a piece of equipment is approximately twelve times the person's body weight. A gymnast on the rings will be subjecting his arms to nine times his own body weight. Fractures usually occur in the legs, arms, wrists, and fingers following heavy falls from equipment or bad landings after vaults. Gymnastics-related dislocations are concentrated in the knees (from falls and landings) and the shoulders and fingers (from accidents on equipment such as the pommel horse, rings, or parallel bars).

The first response in such situations is to make sure that someone calls for paramedic assistance immediately. Any break or dislocation requires hospital treatment. In a good gym, at least one member of the staff will be trained in first aid, and he or she should be called to assist.

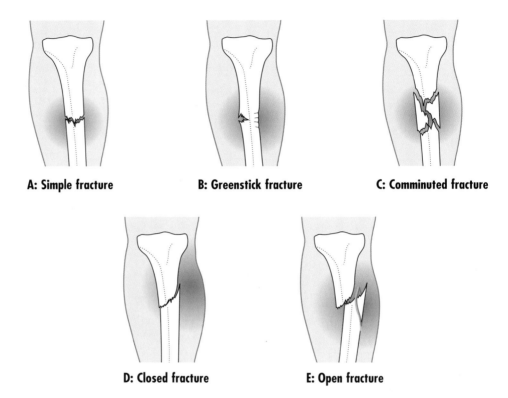

A: Simple fracture   **B: Greenstick fracture**   **C: Comminuted fracture**

D: Closed fracture   **E: Open fracture**

A diagram showing the different ways in which bones can be broken. The most awkward breaks to fix are those where the bone is shattered into fragments (C) or breaks the skin (E).

Treatments for fractures and dislocations vary. For fractures, the first stage in treatment is called "reduction." The doctor places the broken bones in their correct alignment and position, using one of several methods or a combination of methods. Doctors commonly use traction—a gentle pulling action on the broken limb—to draw the bones into their natural alignment. Following this, a plaster or fiberglass cast is usually placed around the injured limb to immobilize it during the healing process. In some cases, what is known as a "functional" cast or brace is applied. This does not immobilize the limb, but permits a limited range of movement in a joint.

In more drastic cases of fracture, surgery may be the only option. Fragments of bone are relocated and pinned into place with surgical screws and/or metal plates attached directly through or onto the bone itself. Sometimes an external frame is also placed around the wound. The metal bars of the frame connect with the pins or screws holding the injury together, providing greater stability for healing.

RETURNING TO TRAINING

Once a fracture is professionally reduced and immobilized, the body will heal itself naturally. Your doctor will tell you when the cast, brace, or frame will be removed, and then you can gently resume training. The key word here is gently: muscles, ligaments, and bones weaken through inactivity, so placing a previously injured limb under heavy stress is liable to result in further injury. Before returning to the gym, do some light weight training and flexibility exercises. Steadily increase the pressure on the injured limb over a period of several weeks until you are back in form.

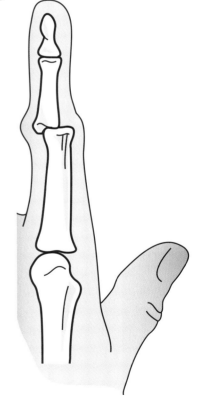

The treatment for a dislocation also begins with reduction. The doctor must relocate the joint into its normal position, and immobilize it. The healing period for dislocation varies according to the amount of damage done to the ligaments and muscles, but the athlete can usually begin light exercise and any recommended physical

A diagram showing a dislocated finger. Dislocated fingers are easily set back in place, but the hand should be given many weeks of rest before strong gripping actions are attempted.

therapy after a four to six week immobilization. However, younger athletes are more vulnerable to redislocation following their initial injury because the damaged ligaments may have weakened or stretched. In fact, around eighty-five percent of athletes aged sixteen to twenty-five, who have suffered a dislocation, suffer another at a later date. If damage is extensive, the recovery period can extend to several months. Sometimes surgery may be required to prevent further injury. As with fractures, dislocations require gradual recovery. Do not overload the joint until strengthening and flexibility exercises have brought it up to par.

OVERUSE INJURIES

Only around fifty percent of gymnastic injuries are caused by sudden accidents. The other half are caused by gradual weakening in the muscle, ligament, bone, or joint, through overuse. There are several warning signs:

- Stiffness in a joint, even when exercising;
- Persistent pain developing in a muscle group or joint;
- Decreasing flexibility, in spite of flexibility training;
- Reduction in the mobility of a limb;
- Weakness in a particular body area;
- Inflammation of a joint or muscle;
- Uneven movement in a joint.

If they are severe, overuse injuries require professional consultation and treatment with a doctor. Be sure to be completely honest with your doctor. Explain your symptoms yourself; do not let anyone else do it for you. Do not succumb to pressure from *anyone* to continue training if the doctor recommends otherwise.

The treatment for this kind of injury, such as painful joints or overworked muscles, is similar to that for a sudden injury. Rest is the first stage. You may not have to stop training entirely, merely abstain from doing the exercise that has caused your injury. If pain is particularly severe, apply ice treatments to reduce the discomfort and to bring down any swelling. A doctor will recommend a program of exercises to help you rehabilitate the injured part. Usually this will not include gymnastics, but will consist of stretching and strengthening exercises designed to build up muscle strength. For joint problems, your doctor may also recommend wearing a support, both during the healing process and for future activities.

SHOULDER DISLOCATION

Shoulder dislocations tend to occur when the arm is lifted high to the side and put under sudden extreme tension.

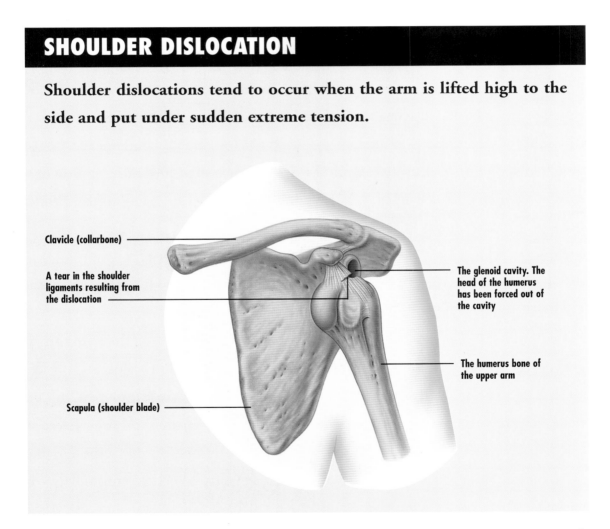

Clavicle (collarbone)

A tear in the shoulder ligaments resulting from the dislocation

The glenoid cavity. The head of the humerus has been forced out of the cavity

The humerus bone of the upper arm

Scapula (shoulder blade)

The onset of gradual injuries is usually a sign of wear and tear, but it may also indicate poor technique. Think about particular movements you repeat over and over. Ankle problems, for example, often result from making repeated pointing figures with the foot. Knee injuries accrue as a result of repeated landings from vaults and from equipment dismounts. Check with your coach to see that you are making these movements correctly, and find out if there is any way to alleviate the problem by varying your technique. Whatever you do, do not ignore the buildup of pain. A minor case may become a career-threatening problem if left untreated.

BACK PROBLEMS

Gymnasts are prone to lower-back strains and injuries. Young female gymnasts are acutely vulnerable, as their routines often involve extreme and repeated curving of the spine. This can result in damage to the spinal vertebrae. Gymnasts age 12–18 years old should be especially careful: if there is a persistent low back pain there is a 25 percent chance of a lower back fracture or stress fracture. Symptoms include:

- A painful ache in the lower back after training;
- Pain extending from the back down into the legs;
- Reduced mobility in the back, preventing twisting and bending actions;
- Tingling or numbness in the arms or legs.

The implications of spinal damage are serious, and may force the gymnast to give up the sport. The initial treatment is to stop training while a doctor provides a full diagnosis (which may involve X-rays and even bone scans). Depending on the condition, the doctor may recommend that you continue training. Exercise can help keep the back flexible and stop it from tightening up, although the movements which caused the problem may have to be temporarily or permanently removed from your routines.

THE HUMAN BACK

The human back is a complex piece of engineering. Its various muscle groups enable a wide range of movement in both the torso and the shoulders.

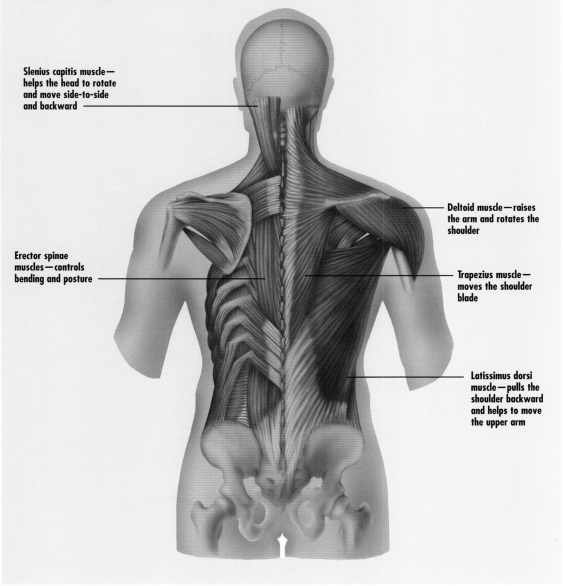

Slenius capitis muscle—helps the head to rotate and move side-to-side and backward

Deltoid muscle—raises the arm and rotates the shoulder

Erector spinae muscles—controls bending and posture

Trapezius muscle—moves the shoulder blade

Latissimus dorsi muscle—pulls the shoulder backward and helps to move the upper arm

A Gymnastics Career

Gymnastics competitors—particularly female gymnasts—are often younger than athletes in almost any other sport. Members of the U.S. National Junior Gymnastics Team can be as young as thirteen years of age.

Gymnastics is a demanding sport, requiring dedication, intelligence, and courage to perform well. Committed gymnasts may aspire to get on the U.S. National Team and represent their country around the world. To go from beginner to Olympic gymnast is extremely difficult and is possible for only the most talented. Yet it can be done and often in a much shorter space of time than it takes to get to national team level in other sports.

JUNIOR OLYMPIC PROGRAM

The Junior Olympic Program (**J.O.P.**) is the first stage on the journey to becoming a national representative in gymnastics. It consists of ten levels for women and seven levels for men. In the men's J.O.P., each level relates to the ability and age of the gymnast. The women's J.O.P. is more focused on ability alone. Gymnasts work their way up the levels by demonstrating an increasing quality of technique in their chosen special fields. To pass the initial levels, they must perform compulsory techniques set by the governing body of gymnastics in the United States, U.S.A. Gymnastics, and score enough points to go on to the

A gymnast demonstrates a rhythmic routine using the ribbon. The judges watch for a ribbon which is constantly moving and always performing prescribed patterns in the air.

Blaine Wilson of the United States prepares to begin his routine on the rings at the 2000 Olympics in Sydney. Wilson began gymnastics at the age of five in 1979 and is one of the most successful U.S. athletes.

next level. In later levels, however, gymnasts can demonstrate techniques of their own choosing.

The criteria for judging each level of the Junior Olympic Program can be tough. Any errors in either style or technique result in points being deducted from the final score. For example, in the men's Class 5 level of the J.O.P., gymnasts have to achieve a base score of 9.3 out of a maximum possible score of 10.0. The routines for men's Class 5 are floor exercise, pommel horse, rings, vault, parallel bars, and horizontal bar. The rules state that:

"If the skills in each sequence are performed with improper technique, or if the gymnast falls on or off the apparatus, has a lapse in form, or any other errors, deductions are taken. One skill may have multiple single deductions. Single deductions range in value as follows: 0.1 (small), 0.2 (medium), 0.3 (large), 0.5 (fall or added part), 1.0 (missing part)."

It is easy to see how quickly a gymnast could lose 0.8 points, thus dropping beneath the 9.3 base score. However, the gymnast can make up lost points through the award of a "Virtuosity Bonus," additional points given for flawless execution of techniques. (Note that the scoring systems of the J.O.P. can vary from year to year.)

One important point to remember is this: even if gymnasts do achieve the score to move up to the next level, they do not have to do so. Going up a level can mean starting at the bottom of the competitive ladder once again in the new level, and also increasing the time spent training. Sometimes this will not suit a gymnast, who may therefore choose to stay at the same level.

TRAINING AND COACHING

Training to pass each level of the J.O.P. requires both diligence and a good coach. Your access to an experienced professional coach depends on whether you have one living in your area. In the past, dedicated gymnasts had to travel widely across the United States to access the best coaches, and families sometimes

Rhythmic gymnast Elena Vitrichenko, of the Ukraine, performs a floor routine at the Olympic Games.

COURTNEY KUPETS

At the age of sixteen, gymnast Courtney Kupets won a gold medal on the asymetric bars at the World Championships in Hungary in 2002. Here, she talks to journalist Luan Peszek about Selection Camp and her gold medal.

Courtney Kupets performs an aerial technique during the EPA Hungary Artistic Gymnastics Championship, 2002. The performance was to bring her first place in the competition.

Q: What was the Selection Camp like?

A: There were just eight of us at the camp. We competed the events we wanted to try to make the World Championships team on. I did bars, beam, and floor.

Q: What did you do when your name was called as a World Championships team member?

A: I was kind of shocked. I didn't know if they would call my name or not. Everyone at the camp was really good.

Q: What were your goals coming into the competition?

A: My first goal was just to make the team. My other goal was to make the finals and possibly a medal.

Q: How does it feel to win a gold medal for the United States?

A: It was a shock and I was surprised. It was really cool.

Q: How will this experience impact your training for next year's World Championships?

A: It makes me want to keep working harder so that I can make the team for next year.

Q: Will there be an advantage next year when you compete in the United States at a World Championships?

A: Definitely. We'll be more used to the equipment and there's no time change issue.

Q: Any advice for young gymnasts?

A: Keep working and push through even if you've had a rough time. Don't give up. Your hard work can pay off.

Q: Have you had to work through some tough times?

A: Yes, just prior to the 2002 U.S. Championships I had some injuries and wasn't sure if I'd even get to go. I'm glad I pushed through it. It's all worth it.

(Reproduced with the kind permission of: www.usa-gymnastics.org, Luan Peszek, Copyright 2003)

had to move in order to put their children near such a coach. Today, the U.S.A. Gymnastics governing body has made life easier for the aspiring gymnast by sending the U.S. National Training Staff across the country to deliver training courses, master classes, and camps. Attending one of these training sessions if it passes through your area is highly recommended. The training staff will give you expert instruction on what is required to advance through the J.O.P.

ELITE PROGRAM

The **Elite Program**, also known as the **International Program**, is a program gymnasts can enter after they have passed through the J.O.P. It is the most intensive program, with gymnasts often training up to thirty-six hours a week. All the training is conducted under the watchful eyes of the U.S.A. Gymnastics Training Team, who pick those individuals capable of representing the United States in major competitions. Those in the Elite Program have the opportunity to compete not just in the U.S. National Championships, but also in international competitions such as the Olympics and World Championships.

Passing the various levels of the J.O.P. is not the only way to enter the Elite Program. There are also fast track courses for young gymnasts who show exceptional talent. Known as the "Future Stars" and "Talent Opportunity Program," these courses consist of a series of preparatory training and competitive events conducted with the highest standards. A gymnast can only find a place on the Elite Program if she or he can meet the exacting demands of these programs. The Elite Program makes assessments of the individual gymnast's talent through a series of exhaustive evaluations. Individuals are also selected to compete in the U.S. National Championships, which are held each year at different places throughout the United States.

Following the National Championships, the U.S. National Team is chosen for competitions such as the World Championships and the Olympics. Most of an international team will be made up of ranked winners from the National Championships or previous international championships, although some unranked gymnasts may take one or two places.

Remember that being selected does not guarantee that you will compete in the Olympics or other international events. The National Team trains incredibly hard all year round, and those on the team must continually prove that they are capable of representing the U.S. at this level.

Few individuals actually become part of the National Team. This does not mean, however, that you should not aspire to get there. Just remember what Steve Whitlock, Director of Internet Services at U.S.A. Gymnastics, says: the main reason young people drop out of gymnastics is that their sport stops being fun. So throw yourself into gymnastics as much as you want to, but also give yourself time for friends, schoolwork, and other hobbies.

Hard training is the only way to success in competition. A professional gymnast will train at least five days a week for up to six hours each day.

Glossary

Asymmetric bars: A piece of apparatus consisting of two parallel bars, one set at 7 feet 10 inches to 8 feet (2.40–2.45 m) high, the other at 5 feet 3 inches to 5 feet 5 inches (1.60–1.65 m) high. The bars are used for routines by women only.

Beam: A beam usually made of aluminum, which is 16 feet 5 inches (5 m) long and 4 inches (10 cm) wide. It is used in women's gymnastics.

Cold compress: A piece of material soaked in cold water or packed with ice and wrapped around an injury to reduce swelling.

Dislocation: An injury in which a joint is pulled out of its normal alignment.

Elite Program: A training program in the United States, from which national and international competitors are selected.

FIG: *Fédération Internationale Gymnastique*, the main organization overseeing international gymnastics.

Floor exercise: Gymnastic routines performed without stationary equipment on a section of matting 40 x 40 feet (12 x 12 m).

Hamstrings: The group of three large muscles set at the back of the thigh.

High bar: See Horizontal Bar.

Horizontal bar: A single bar set 8 feet 4 inches (2.55 m) above the ground and used for men's acrobatic displays.

International Program: See Elite Program.

J.O.P.: Abbreviation for Junior Olympic Program, a program in the United States for the development of young athletes.

Ligament: A short band of tough body tissue, which connects bones or holds together joints.

Parallel bars: A piece of equipment in men's gymnastics consisting of two bars set 5 feet 9 inches (1.75 m) off the ground.

Physical therapy: The treatment of an injury or illness using physical techniques such as massage and stretching, rather than medicines or surgery.

Pommel horse: Used in men's gymnastics, this narrow wooden or steel box is 5 feet 3 inches (1.6 m) long and covered with leather or synthetic material, featuring two grip handles in the center.

Rhythmic gymnastics: Dancelike athletic routines on a mat using hand-held equipment such as ribbons, balls, and hoops.

Rings: Equipment used in men's gymnastics; two wooden or plastic rings hang 7 feet 5 inches (2.25 m) from the ground by chains from a metal frame.

R.O.M.: Abbreviation for Range of Movement.

Salto: A flip or somersault in which the feet travel over the head while the body rotates itself.

Spotter: Someone who assists a gymnast in doing a technique during training.

Vaulting horse: A piece of equipment used in vaulting techniques; in men's gymnastics, it is 4 feet 5 inches (1.35 m) high; in women's gymnastics, 4 feet 1 inch (1.25 m) high.

Further Information

FURTHER INFORMATION

To learn about gymnastic skills: www.drillsandskills.com

For a global view of gymnastics: www.gymworld.com/home.php3

Inside Gymnastics magazine online: www.insidegymnastics.com

International Gymnastics magazine online: www.intlgymnast.com

U.S.A. Gymnastics: www.usa-gymnastics.org

The Web sites listed on this page were active at the time of publication. The publisher is not responsible for Web sites that have changed their address or discontinued operation since the date of publication. The publisher will review and update the Web sites upon each reprint.

FURTHER READING

Feeney, Rik. *Gymnastics: A Guide for Parents and Athletes.* New York: McGraw-Hill/Contemporary, 1995.

Jackman, Joan and Shannon Miller. *Superguides: Gymnastics.* New York: Dorling Kindersley, 2000.

Mitchell, Debbie et al. *Teaching Fundamental Gymnastics Skills.* Champaign, Illinois: Human Kinetics, 2002.

U.S.A. Gymnastics. *I Can Do Gymnastics: Essential Skills for Beginning Gymnasts.* New York: McGraw-Hill, 1993.

Vidmar, Peter, et al. *Sport Psychology Library: Gymnastics.* Morgantown, West Virginia: Fitness Info Tech, 2000.

THE AUTHOR

Dr. Chris McNab is a writer and editor specializing in sports, survival, and other human-performance topics. He has written more than twenty-five books, and recent publications include *Survival First Aid, Martial Arts for People with Disabilities, Living Off the Land,* and *How to Pass the SAS Selection Course.* Chris lives in South Wales, U.K.

THE CONSULTANTS

Susan Saliba, Ph.D., is a senior associate athletic trainer and a clinical instructor at the University of Virginia in Charlottesville, Virginia. A certified athletic trainer and licensed physical therapist, Dr. Saliba provides sports medicine care, including prevention, treatment, and rehabilitation for the varsity athletes at the University. Dr. Saliba holds dual appointments as an Assistant Professor in the Curry School of Education and the Department of Orthopaedic Surgery. She is a member of the National Athletic Trainers' Association's Educational Executive Committee and its Clinical Education Committee.

Eric Small, M.D., a Harvard-trained sports medicine physician, is a nationally recognized expert in the field of sports injuries, nutritional supplements, and weight management programs. He is author of *Kids & Sports* (2002) and is Assistant Clinical Professor of Pediatrics, Orthopedics, and Rehabilitation Medicine at Mount Sinai School of Medicine in New York. He is also Director of the Sports Medicine Center for Young Athletes at Blythedale Children's Hospital in Valhalla, New York. Dr. Small has served on the American Academy of Pediatrics Committee on Sports Medicine for the past six years, where he develops national policy regarding children's medical issues and sports.

Index

Page numbers in *italics* refer to photographs and illustrations.